T0127024

Tracks of a
Fellow Struggler

Tracks of a Fellow Struggler

Living and Growing through Grief

JOHN R. CLAYPOOL

FOREWORD BY
RUSSELL J. LEVENSON JR.

Morehouse Publishing
NEW YORK

Revised Edition published in 1995 by Insight Press, New Orleans.
2004, 2019 Editions published by
Morehouse Publishing
An imprint of Church Publishing
19 East 34th Street
New York, NY 10016
www.churchpublishing.org

Cover art by Roger Hutchison
Cover design by Beth Oberholtzer

A record of this book is available from the Library of Congress.

ISBN-13: 978-1-64065-311-5 (paperback)
ISBN-13: 978-0-8192-2747-8 (ebook)

Printed in the United States of America

To
Laura Lue

a beautiful child
and
in the end
a brave one

Contents

Foreword to the 2019 Edition

"Yea though I walk through the valley of the shadow of death, I will fear no evil; for thou art with me." —*Psalm 23:4*

Nowhere in the Bible will we find a promise that life will come without sorrow or pain, trial or tribulation; what is promised to the one who has eyes to see is a companion "through" to the other side. Perhaps in no moment of life do we need such a companion more than in the valley of the shadow of death.

God sends companions in all kinds of ways: a piece of music, the dawn of a new day, an unexpected memory, a listening ear, the warm embrace of a loved one. Those in vocational ministry are called to be companions through pastoral care and the sacraments, and in what John Clay-pool often called "the preaching moment." How much more potent is that moment when the preacher knows the deep heart of the message they seek to share.

Tracks of a Fellow Struggler is such a companion through death's shadowy valley. Four sermons prayerfully crafted by a master wordsmith and a powerful preacher. Four frank and honest words shared not to diminish the power of grief but to soften its blow by the hope offered in the Christian faith. This book is not a miraculous work that will do away with grief. It is medicine for the grieving soul.

I first met John in the summer of 1987. I was not yet ordained, but I was interested in exploring a call to the Episcopal priesthood. John learned of my interest and called me for lunch. I knew virtually nothing of his story, of his well-deserved notoriety. I did not know about his written works, and I did not know how his ministry, his theology, and his life were changed by the death of his beloved daughter Laura Lue.

I was young, naïve, self-centered—perhaps even cocky—but John and I hit it off from the first moment. He brought me onto his staff as a layperson before I started seminary. He witnessed patiently and coached me lovingly through my earliest foibles, errors, and sins. He was more than my rector. He was my spiritual director and, in every sense of the word, a spiritual father.

I could write a book on the things I loved about him. Among those traits that were much beloved were his humility, his humor, and his joy. John loved a great laugh. I suspect I laughed more in my years of working with John than in all my other years of ministry combined. I share this insight into his humor because when I learned the story of Laura Lue—a story he told me dozens of times, from dozens of different perspectives—I found it hard to square such a tragic season of life with the disciple of joy I knew.

In the pages that follow, you will see how God moved with John through that valley. Because God did, John's words still travel with us. He holds nothing back. In the third sermon, he heartbreakingly lifts the veil of his pain: "I perhaps need to confess to you that at times in the last few months I have been tempted to conclude that this whole existence of ours is utterly absurd." Anyone who has experienced the death of a loved one, perhaps especially the death of a child, would have to, at some point, ask this kind of question.

Here is a book that allows you to question God's motives, God's power—even, perhaps, God's love. It allows you because John did just that. You will find no attempt to rush you to a finish line with grief in these pages because, as I witnessed in John's life, grief ebbs and flows, but it never fully goes away.

I can still see in my mind's eye, tears welling up each of the many times that John shared with me what he felt the day Laura Lue died. "I had prepared for it for so long, but when the end came . . . when she took that last breath . . . I just could not believe it . . . I simply did not know how I could go on." Fortunately, for all of us, John did find a way. But it was not an easy or a smooth journey.

John Claypool could have stopped praying, put his Bible aside. John could have given up his calling, welcomed the bitterness that can often engulf the soul that feels robbed of a loved one. But John did none of these things. Instead, through tears and struggle, pain and prayer, in the same way Jacob wrestled with God and would not turn loose until God blessed him, John wrestled.

One of John's favorite sayings was, "Despair is presumptuous." It was not a pithy one-liner. It was something he fully experienced. In the fourth sermon, "Learning to

Handle Grief," John wrote, "The basic issue in grief is never a rational explanation anyway. What matters is the nature of life itself and the One who gives it." No easy explanations. Instead, John discovered in the depths of heartache a compass that points the struggling traveler in the path of hope, by the grace and mercy of the Lord Jesus, on a journey from heartache to gratitude.

The first time I walked into John's office, I saw a brass plaque in the center of his desk with three simple words: "Life is Gift." From the day we met until the day John left this life for the next almost twenty years later, he embodied those words. When we met, I was a young husband to my wife, Laura, and we had the first of our three children. John and his wife, Ann, took us both under their wings and became godparents to our children. He encouraged us to continue onto ministry.

After my ordination years later, I was blessed to come back on and serve as one of his associate priests. When I was called to my first post as a rector, John supported me and preached at my institution. When I was called to my second rectorship, John preached there as well. Over two decades, we prayed together, talked endlessly, shared meals and vacations. John was a critic only when invited to be, and even then he was always compassionate and gentle. To those of us blessed by his extensive gifts, he effortlessly served as an engaged listener and a consummate comforter. He was my brother, my confessor, my friend. I share my personal connection with John because not once in nearly two decades did I see anything in John's manner, words, or dealings with others that were anything other than the words and deeds of one who truly believed that life—all of life—was, in fact, a gift.

I remember one day I saw John following a preaching opportunity he had in Washington, DC. He bubbled over with joy as he told me that he had been contacted by a young woman who had gone to elementary school with Laura Lue. She saw that John was preaching and wanted to see if they could meet. John did not hesitate—he took it as an opportunity to grow even more fully into life. He said, "She was the same age as Laura Lue, so of course as I reflected on the time we shared, I wondered what my daughter would have become if she had remained in this life. What would she have looked like? What career might she have chosen?" He did not collapse into grief but gave way into wonder.

John taught me that a large part of the gift of life was growing, and that stagnant existence was an abandonment of that holy gift. I was struck by how John relished meeting new people even well into his later years. He enjoyed a good meal and never held back from trying new things. He was always reading, was an avid athlete, and enjoyed the craft of teaching and preaching. John taught me the importance of leading with love and empathy. He taught me the value of forgiving others and asking for their forgiveness. He also showed me the path toward forgiving myself for my own mistakes and sins; not resting in forgiveness alone, but turning over my shadow self, as John would say, my bruises and broken places to the transforming power of the Holy Spirit.

Then came his own journey toward the end. I remember when Ann called Laura and me to say that John had been diagnosed with multiple myeloma. John was only offered hope of remission, but no hope of a cure. John's response? "I wonder what God will teach me through this journey?"

It was a long battle, but John did go into remission. He was in the hospital in Atlanta toward the end of his treatment when I called him. I told him that my son, his godson, and I would be passing through town on our way to a white-water-rafting trip in the Tennessee mountains. John asked if I would come by and bring him communion.

John was visibly weaker, but he was on his way to fuller life. We talked and, as always, laughed. He did not obsess about his condition but kept asking about my son, my other two children, my wife, and how things were going in my new ministry in Florida.

We held hands. We prayed the Lord's Prayer. We shared communion. As we came to the point of offering our thanks for the heavenly meal, we both got a bit weepy. I finished by anointing John's head with oil, praying for him, and then kissing him on his forehead. Our time came to an end, but not without an exchange of smiles and "I love yous." It would be the last time I would see John. It would be the last time he received Holy Communion.

A few weeks later, early one morning, Laura woke me to tell me that John, though in remission, had weakened in the wake of his treatment and the body that had served him and others so well for seventy-four years had released him into eternal life.

I can honestly say that not a day goes by that I do not miss John. I wish I could pick up the phone and call him, or sit down with him for a great meal, or bow my head with him for a good prayer. I wish he were still here. But what he taught me was to find my way through grief, not by being swallowed by what is no longer but by holding fast with gratitude for what was, what has been, and what will be.

Days later, countless numbers of people gathered for his funeral at St. Luke's in Birmingham, Alabama, where he had served for so many years. The number of clergy present was almost too great to count. He had asked that a few of the younger clergy who had served under his leadership participate in his funeral, and that his long-time friend, The Very Rev. Dr. Sam Lloyd preach the homily. It was a word of hope, as well it should have been. The theme from beginning to end was simple: "Life is Gift." Several times throughout the sermon, Sam paused and invited the congregation to say those three words that John lived so well and shared so liberally.

John had requested that I read the Gospel lesson. He chose a portion of John 14 where Jesus says to his disciples, "Do not let your hearts be troubled. Believe in God, believe also in me. In my Father's house there are many dwelling places. If it were not so would I have told you that I go to prepare a place for you? And if I go and prepare a place for you, I will come again and will take you to myself, so that where I am, there you may be also."

I am not exactly sure of the moment when John's grief began that first turn toward gratitude over loss, but whenever it was, in that moment I think God deposited even more solidly into John's spiritual DNA that peace that passes all understanding. When you were with John, your heart had a hard time being troubled—I think this was because his faith was rooted in an absolute certainty of the power of the resurrection of Jesus of Nazareth and that power confirmed the deep truth that in God's hands, life does not end. It merely changes. The promise of Jesus is a promise to us all that in lifting our hearts to his redemptive power and love, we too will rise because—to use one of John's favorite metaphors for Jesus—in trusting our life and death, as well as the deaths of our loved ones, to the Great Alchemist, we can rest assured that the words "The End" will never roll across the screen of the saga that is our sacred journey through this world to the next.

I have now been an ordained priest for nearly three decades, and I cannot tell you how many copies of *Tracks of a Fellow Struggler* I have shared with others. I have known the deaths of loved ones, and I have known grief. I have been blessed to sit with many at the moment of death, to officiate at the funerals of hundreds more, and to pray with perhaps thousands left to their own struggle. Without exception, John's words have been the best companion for those trying to find their way to a place of joy, of peace—a place where all of life, is, as John described, a gift.

It is a hope-filled reminder that all we have is gift, and that gift, lived in the grip of the grace of Almighty God means that when this life comes to its natural end, life merely changes form, and the gift becomes more holy, and full, and precious than it ever was before.

John closes this beloved volume with these words: "No matter what the form of grief, we can win through and become deeper and richer human beings. No one ever said this would be easy to do, but believe me, it is possible. . . . So, come people of sorrow, acquainted with grief, let us all follow him and be blessed."

The journey of grief is not one you have to make alone. Turn the page and follow the tracks of a fellow struggler from despair to hope, from sadness to strength, from death to life, allowing what seems to be an end to become a new beginning. Life—all of life—is gift.

RUSS LEVENSON JR.
Autumn, 2019

Foreword

The element of testimony, long strangely silent in the pulpits of America, has suddenly sprung into full intensity in the preaching of John Claypool. To him preaching has long ceased to be the making of pretty, neatly trimmed religious speeches remembered more for their entertainment value and their clever phrase-making than for their declaration of the whole counsel of God. Preaching for John Claypool is the disciplined confession of the preacher of his and his people's travail and celebration in conversation with God on a face-to-face basis—questions, complaints, agonies, ecstasies, and all.

The contents of this book are records of the prophetic utterance of John Claypool as he spoke with the congregation of the Crescent Hill Baptist Church in Louisville, Kentucky, of his terror, grief, loss, comfort, and consecration in the face of the death of his ten-year-old child, Laura Lue.

I participated in this community of suffering, not as a member of the church, but as a member of the immediate community of which the church is a part, and as students of mine served as chaplains on the staff of the hospital where she suffered her fatal illness. And I listened while physicians alongside of whom I worked in the hospitals of the community recounted in awestruck terms their experience of having heard these sermons. They gave thanks for the way in which John Claypool made them acutely aware of the presence of God as well as the dark mysteries of the shrouds of grief.

In a different way I myself was facing during the same time span the imminent possibility of the death of one of my sons. He fought for a year in some of the bloodiest engagements of the Vietnam War as a machinegunner on a Navy river assault boat. I was spared having to see my son die, because he came home alive, unscarred, and mentally strong. The fact that he is alive and Laura Lue is dead perplexes me with the alternatives, among others, of fatalism, luck, being specially favored by God. I have had to conclude that in the instance either of death or of life, nothing can separate us from the love of God in Christ Jesus. Grief slams us in the face with the perils of idolatry of those we have tenderly cared for, strongly defended, and sacrificially provided for as parents.

Yet, in John Claypool's sermons the crystal clarity of the supremacy of our loving worship of the Lord Jesus Christ moves through the darkness to give us strength just when we least expect it. Shining through John Claypool's sermon "Life Is Gift" is the deep meaning of charisma—a word that is being badly mauled with distortion today—as the sense of awe, gratitude, and dedicated being that comes from being redeemed from destruction to creativity. "The Basis of Hope" is in God as we become disciples, learners, students of the handling of grief.

This is the stuff of which authentic John Claypool witnesses to his people and to you and to me as we read and reread this book.

WAYNE E. OATES

Preface

This little book reflects my own encounter with the realities of terminal illness and death and the grief that follows.

It is written from the inside of events, not the outside. For almost two decades, I had served as a pastor and often participated in the drama of suffering and death, but it was always happening to someone else. I could sympathize, but never really empathize. However, no one can live on this earth very long without being initiated into the fraternity of the bereaved. The Darkness moved closer and closer into the circle of my being while I sat beside my father-in-law's bed as he died. Then shortly afterward it neared again when the wife of one of my closest friends slipped in the Mystery. Yet it was not until part of my own flesh and blood—my eight-year-old daughter, Laura Lue—was diagnosed with acute leukemia that "my time came" and I was thrust inside the trauma of living with and through the mystery of dying.

Three of the four sermons on the following pages were born out of this experience. Laura Lue lived eighteen months and ten days from the time of diagnosis, just a shade longer than the national average for leukemia at that time. During those months I shared these sermons with the Crescent Hill Baptist Church in Louisville, Kentucky—the first one eleven days after we first learned of the disease, a second after her first major relapse some nine months later, and the third several weeks after she had died. The last sermon was preached in Broadway Baptist Church in Fort Worth, Texas, some three years later and represents a reflective overview of the whole grief process. These sermonic efforts constitute the main part of the book, although I have tried to sketch in the background events that formed the setting of each of the sharings.

As one would expect, sermons of this nature evoked a variety of response. Some people were frankly offended at the notes of ambiguity and anger that I openly acknowledged. They obviously felt that preachers were to deal with "answers" and not "questions." One seminary professor even murmured that the third sermon bordered on heresy. At that same time, many other people acknowledged being helped by some, if not all, of these words.

In the four years since this experience, I have had numerous requests for copies of these sermons to share with other sufferers, and many indications of their fruitfulness. It is on the strength of these responses that I have moved to share them more widely in this form.

It has taken this long to get to the place I could handle this material without overwhelming pain. Just like a broken leg, a broken heart heals slowly and cannot stand much touching right after the break. Then, too, I needed a while to see for myself how things would "live out" after the silence of death became a permanent part of my ongoing. What I said in the extremes of the agony was as true as I knew how to say it at that time, but I needed to see how well such insight stood up under further living. I am now willing to affirm that the ground that sustained me then is still firm enough to support the weight of life. I am more convinced than ever that the hope of biblical religion is authentic vision and realistic perspective.

There is no way to acknowledge fully the many human sources that were used by the Mystery to make this pilgrimage what it was for me. At the intellectual level, two writers bequeathed great gifts of insight—George A. Buttrick in his volume *God, Pain, and Evil* and Gerhard Von Rad in his commentary on *Genesis*. The congregation of the Crescent Hill Church in Louisville carried our whole family through this valley with unbelievable tenderness and support, and will remain forever an affectionate part of our lives. My staff colleagues at that time—Howard Hovde, Temp Sparkman, Arnold Epley, Wendell Brigance, and Bill Amos—"took up the slack" for me again and again and were of great individual support. So were the two physicians who tried so heroically to win the battle—Owen Ogden and Donald Kmetz. My special friend and confidant, William E. Hull, also helped me tremendously by filling the pulpit on several occasions when I could not preach and by speaking so movingly of "The Sound of Silence" at Laura Lue's funeral. My family was also of great support. Most of all, however, I was helped by my only other child, my son, Rowan, who steadfastly called me on to life and away from a preoccupation with the tomb.

In a conversation soon after the initial diagnosis, Temp Sparkman said, in essence: "Those of us who have not been there wonder what it is like out there in the Darkness. Can you tell us?" The answer is, of course, yes and no. I can only share the glimpse of things that came to me from my particular way of looking. These words make no attempt to say everything for everyone. They represent the most important things I learned down where the valley is dark but where there also is light on beyond and out ahead.

Since eventually we all become "persons of sorrow, acquainted with grief," I hope these tracks of a fellow struggler will furnish companionship and hope for you.

JOHN R. CLAYPOOL

CHAPTER ONE

The Basis of Hope

She was a bright, exuberant child, full of life and joy as she finished the second grade and participated in two recitals in one day—a Suzuki violin performance on Saturday morning and a ballet recital that evening.

The next day she seemed tired, and we attributed it to her hyperactivity. But she stayed tired, and then her ankle began to swell and finally the pediatrician sent us to a specialist at Children's Hospital where on the third day we heard the words "*acute leukemia*."

That was on a Wednesday, and I made no attempt to preach the following Sunday. But then the first treatments began to take effect, Laura Lue went into an immediate "remission" or return to normalcy, and eleven days after the initial news, this is what I shared with the congregation.

We know that in everything God works for good with those who love him, who are called according to his purpose. For those whom he foreknew he also predestined to be conformed to the image of his Son, in order that he might be the first-born among many brethren. And those whom he predestined he also called; and those whom he called he also justified; and those whom he justified he also glorified.

What then shall we say to this? If God is for us, who is against us? He who did not spare his own Son but gave him up for us all, will he not also give us all things with him? Who shall bring any charge against God's elect? It is God who justifies; who is to condemn? Is it Christ Jesus, who died, yes, who was raised from the dead, who is at the right hand of God, who indeed intercedes for us? Who shall separate us from the love of Christ? Shall tribulation, or distress, or persecution, or famine, or nakedness, or peril, or sword? As it is written,

> *"For Thy sake we are being killed all the day long;*
> *we are regarded as sheep to be slaughtered."*

No, in all these things we are more than conquerors through him who loved us. For I am sure that neither death, nor life, nor angels, nor principalities, nor things present, nor things to come, nor powers, nor height, nor depth, nor anything else in all creation will be able to separate us from the love of God in Christ Jesus our Lord.

Romans 8:28–39

It has never been easy for me to stand in this place and try to preach a sermon, but I must confess to you this morning that it is doubly difficult. As many of you know, the last two weeks have been full of trauma for me and my family. During these days my eight-year-old daughter was diagnosed as having leukemia, and we have been called upon to shift very swiftly from the shock and numbness that first comes from such a disclosure to the task of learning to care for her and now to live with a degree of normalcy in the shadow of such an enormity.

Needless to say, not all of this has been accomplished. There are still great areas of this whole experience about which I cannot speak. It has been hard to think, much less concentrate significantly in these last few days. Thus the prospect of preaching a sermon is rather formidable.

But all of this is only one side of the picture. Long before this happened to me, I had come to the conclusion, that it was the nature of God to speak to us in the language of events, and that it was the nature of the Church for human beings to share with each other what they thought they had heard God say in the things that had happened to them. There is no evading the fact that I have just been through a dark place, but it has not been totally black or without its flashes of light. Therefore, difficult as it may be, there is something I want to share with you, my family in Christ. Please do not expect any great homiletical master-piece. Do not look for any tightly reasoned, original crea-tion. Rather, see me this morning as your burdened and broken brother, limping back into the family circle to tell you something of what I learned out there in the darkness.

The first thing I have to share may surprise you a bit, but I must in all honesty confess it, and that is: *I have found no answers to the deepest questions of this experience.* When I first heard the diagnosis and went out alone to cry, I asked the same things anyone would ask: "Why has this happened? Why do little girls get leukemia? Why is there leukemia at all? Why is there sickness and suffering and pain in a world that is supposed to be the creation of an all-good and an all-powerful God?"

Such questions are age-old, and I searched the pages of the Bible and my books of theology and my memory and my Christian experience, and I found no neat and tidy answers to lay them to rest. I was already familiar with most of the attempted solutions to this problem of evil and pain, and every one of them left something to be desired. Up to this moment, nowhere have I found any single answer that settles all the questions or accounts for all the nuances of this tragic occurrence. The enigma remains what it has been from the beginning—a dark mystery for which there is no satisfactory explanation.

I would be untrue to myself if I did not openly admit this to you. However, to stop at this point would also be untrue. The same honesty that prompts me not to over-claim, prompts me not to underclaim either. And while I have not found any total answer, I have found three things that have been of tremendous value to me in the last two weeks.

One of these is the challenge to go on living even though I have no answer or any complete explanation. The

Bible arranges life and thought in just that sequence. First, we are called on to live passionately and openly and then to use our minds to try to understand and interpret what we have experienced. In this way life moves on and whatever insight is possible is born. If we turn the whole process around and try to put understanding before the living of life, however, everything freezes and we become immobilized.

I found this to be so in the first hours after I heard the diagnosis. The ultimate question "why?" leaped to my mind almost immediately, and, as I have told you, I could find no adequate solution to this enigma. But alongside that question were also several concrete realities—a little girl who was sick and whose course of treatment needed to be charted; other loved ones who needed to be comforted, and a son who needed to be reassured that he was important too. I could have turned away from all of these immediate necessities and said, "Until I find an intellectual answer for all of this, I will not move a step or do anything." But that would have been criminal neglect and the closing off of the one avenue whereby I might gain insight.

Harry Emerson Fosdick once wrote that "persons can put off making up their minds, but they cannot put off making up their lives." That statement has all the realism of the Bible behind it. The business of making up one's life, concretely and directly, is more basic than intellectualizing abstractly about it. And not only that, it is the way we were meant to learn. Making up our minds is not something we can do before we experience anything of life; it comes as we experience it, through experience, after experience.

Centuries ago a philosopher named Descartes climbed into a stove and determined to think out life before he acted. When he finally came to the conclusion "I think, therefore I am," he set the whole direction of modern Western thought. His was a fatal mistake, however, for he reversed the true relation of living and thinking and "got the cart before the horse."

It was the same mistake that Adam and Eve made back in the Garden of Eden. God spread the whole creation out before them like a banquet table and invited them to participate in it fully. They were to eat, drink, work, multiply; that is, to live passionately. But instead of immersing themselves in life, they turned rather to the tree of the knowledge of good and evil, the symbol of the Ultimate explanation of all things that belonged to God alone, and lusted after it. In other words, before they lived they wanted to know all the answers, whereas God had ordained that knowledge was to come through and by and after experience.

This temptation to think life rather than to live it is always a dead-end street. Instead of saying, "I think, therefore I am," Descartes should have come out of his stove and exclaimed, "I am, therefore I think," This is the sequence in which life and thought should always be placed. We do not first get all the answers and then live in light of our understanding. We must rather plunge into life—meeting what we have to meet and experiencing what we have to experience—and in the light of living try to understand. If insight comes at all, it will not be before, but only through and after experience.

This emphasis of the Bible really helped me move on last week when I found myself in the depths. Instead of sitting down to brood and question and refusing to budge until I had an answer, I plunged headlong into what had to be faced. I got on with the business of "making up my life," with the hope that in so doing the making up of the mind might later come. The Bible gave me no answer, but it did challenge me to face up to the situation and move on into the darkness.

The second thing the Bible and my faith gave me was a stern warning to beware of superficiality and quick labeling, of jumping to the wrong conclusions. If the Bible says anything to us about life, it is that this existence of ours is a deep and complex and mysterious affair. Just as icebergs show only a fraction of themselves above the surface, so events are always more than they appear to be at first glance. More is going on in every moment than meets the eye, and the Bible always cautions us against pronouncing too quickly, "This is all bad"; "this is all good"; "this is hopeless"; "this is the end."

I really needed this kind of safeguard in the past few weeks, for my temptation was to conclude that all pain is evil, all sickness bad, leukemia equals certain death, and thus all will be lost. The testimony of the Bible slowed me down by saying; "Wait a moment. You can't always judge an event by its first appearance, any more than you can judge the content of a package by its wrapping. Be patient. Let events run their course. God is not through with anything yet. Who knows what might yet unfold out of all of this process?"

The Old Testament story of Joseph and his traumatic life was of great comfort to me here. All though this saga "a double agenda" was at work. The outward manifestation was always at first deceptive of the deeper realities that were moving. For example, as a lad Joseph was the cocky and spoiled favorite son of his father, and the only things his brothers could see in him and his dreams was an intolerable arrogance. But Joseph had in him the potential to be a great leader, and what they mistook for something evil was actually the first appearing of these significant gifts.

The brothers' hatred led them to sell Joseph into slavery and send him far away to Egypt—an act that bore every mark of sheer evil. Yet look at what resulted. The rigors of slavery in Egypt developed the character of Joseph in ways that might never have occurred under the pampering of a doting old father. And what is more, the brothers' "evil" act eventually catapulted Joseph into a position where, decades later, he was able to save his family from starvation.

Reading this story always reminds me of the mysterious depth of events and causes me "to put on the brakes" when I rush out to define something as "good" or "bad" or "evil" or "hopeless." How do I know, finite as I am, the full import of events?

A few years ago I would have pronounced "good" the fortune of a lowly mechanic who won the Irish sweepstakes and overnight became rich. Nevertheless, just the other day I read an account of what instant wealth had done to this man's life. He had lost his desire to work. Separated from his wife and alienated from his children, he said quite flatly: "I now look on the day I won that money as the darkest day in my life." By the same token I would always be tempted to judge a heart attack an evil and dreadful thing, full of darkness. Contrary to that opinion, however, Jesse Stuart, the poet-teacher, wrote a whole book to proclaim that his coronary had proved to be a great blessing to his overcrowded life and occasioned "the year of his rebirth."

My point is that the Bible is right in warning us against living too much on the surface or by appearances only. It reminds us quite explicitly that despair is always presumptuous. How do we know what lies in the Great Not Yet or how some present "evil" may work itself out as a blessing in disguise?

This has become my outlook so far as my little daughter is concerned. I have not embraced despair as to her future, nor pronounced as hopeless her particular situation. After all, she might be the one on whom the long-awaited cure for leukemia will be discovered. God may heal her or, even in taking her, do something magnificent we cannot now envision. At any rate, the Bible gives me a depth perspective on events and bids me "to wait on the Lord" and be patient before I label any experience or close the door of hope. Despair is presumption, pure and simple, a going beyond what the facts at hand should warrant. Who am I to speak dogmatically about what lies hidden out in the not-already-experienced?

Such a reminder of depth and mystery is a valuable gift indeed, but I feel the greatest gift of all is the vision of God that breaks through the events of the Bible. Here, in contrast to the presumption of despair, is the basis of positive hope. And the Christian faith goes even farther—it depicts a God from whom something positive can be expected. Rather than remaining neutral toward the possibilities of the future, we have grounds for hope in what God is.

Time will not permit a full application of theology to tragedy, but two facets of God's Being stand out. One is God's acquaintance with evil and grief and suffering.

The gods of other religions seem content to live on the other side of the sky, but not the God of the Bible. Again and again God came into the circle of the people in the Old Testament; and then in the fullness of time, God sent his Son, made in the image of humankind, to live totally and completely among us. That Son made no attempt to evade the horror and pain of life. In fact, in the Apostles' Creed the only verb used to describe his life is the word "suffer." Between being "conceived by the Holy Spirit and born of the Virgin Mary," and "being crucified, dead, and buried," there is just one phrase: "He suffered under Pontius Pilate." The Son of God, "the Word made flesh," was a Person of sorrows and acquainted with grief. In him, God has drawn very close and understands from within the whole agony of life.

We do feel a certain kinship with those who have experienced what we are experiencing, and the God who came in Christ establishes just such a bond of closeness. During World War II, just after word had arrived that an only son had been killed in battle, a minister was called to the home of his parents. The father, half in grief and half in rage, blurted out as soon as the minister arrived: "I want to know, where was God when my son was being killed?"

The minister thought a long time and then replied softly: "I guess God was where God was while His Boy was being killed." This word had a revolutionary impact on the distraught man, for it brought God out of remoteness and into that circle as a grieving Companion.

This bond of closeness has meant more to me than I can say in these last days. As I have stood and watched my child suffer, I have thought to myself that I could not stand it. But then I remembered what God went through with his Child. Suddenly I was not alone any longer, but companioned by Another who seemed to say: "I know, O how I know. For you see, I watched my Child suffer too. I understand." Believe me, out there in the darkness this companionship of understanding really helps.

The other thing that is so significant to me about the biblical God is what God did about pain and evil. God not only watched God's child suffer; God brought him through it, even death! God took the pain and gathered it up unto his purpose! The raising of Christ Jesus from the dead is not only the greatest deed of the Bible; it is our basis of hope in the midst of tragedy. Here is what God can do with the events that the powers of evil thrust against him. God can bring us through, raise us even from death, and then turn that evil "inside out" and transform it into something good.

The killing of Jesus had many motives behind it, but only one purpose—and that was to defeat God. All the darkness of evil converged on that spot to do God in; but what resulted? Jesus survived! Three days later he was back on earth as real as ever. What is more, the Cross itself was gathered up and became the instrument of God instead of an instrument of evil. Just as in the Old Testament little David stunned Goliath and then used the giant's own sword finally to defeat him, so God in the resurrection stunned evil and then seized the cross from the scabbard of Calvary to use as a power unto salvation instead of destruction. The twin events of Cross and Resurrection are the basis of hope in the face of evil. Evil cannot overcome God; God has overcome it—and not only overcome it, but so transformed it that it can become God's instrument and be used by God for good.

This is the bedrock of my own hope. What God could do for his Boy in the midst of suffering I dare to believe God can do for my girl. I am staking my life on the belief that our present calamity will not end in darkness. Laura Lue may suffer, she may even die, but God will bring her through and us also. And out of whatever happens God will not be overcome but will somehow turn this evil to good purpose and in it all bring light out of darkness.

This, then, is what I have come to share with you as a burdened brother. I have no answer as to why this happened, or why such events should occur in our world, but out of the biblical perspective I have received the challenge to move forward courageously and not get paralyzed in intellectualizing. I am called to live in order to know rather than trying to know in order to live. I have also been warned against superficiality and the tendency to conclude prematurely on the basis of first appearances. Reality is deep and slow and mysterious. How can I yet define as good or evil or hopeless what lies in The Great Not Yet? Despair is presumptuous. But best of all: I have a vision of God, who has come close enough in his Son to understand, and who is powerful enough and resourceful enough to endure the worst that evil can do and then out of it bring the best. It is true I do not have an answer that ties everything into a neat and tidy package for me, but I do have enough light to move on and to give thanks and to form a basis of hope. And this is what I intend to do, by God's help and yours—to offer this whole experience up to God and wait upon God and be patient. And I do not believe I shall be disappointed.

I was deeply moved this week by an observation of Dr. George Buttrick's concerning the Dead Sea in Palestine. Again and again as a sermon illustration I have heard the Dead Sea compared unfavorably with the Sea of Galilee, which is fresh and sparkling and full of fish, while the Dead Sea is salty and no fish can live in it. The usual point is that the Jordan River flows *through* the Sea of Galilee, but only flows *into* the Dead Sea because there is no outlet. Dr. Buttrick concedes the truth of this point about life through giving but then goes on to identify another truth of which I had never thought. He claims the Dead Sea does have an outlet—the upward one, toward the sky. Across the centuries, as it has surrendered itself to the sun, a residue of potash has built up and remains along its shores. Potash is a different form of life than the water in which fish can live, and is a main ingredient of fertilizer. Engineers have estimated that if the potash around the Dead Sea could be mined and distributed, there would be enough there to fertilize the whole surface of the earth for at least five years. The point is, life never comes to a complete dead end. When no outlet is open except surrender to the sky in helplessness, even this response is not without its positive residue, for out of it can come the miracle of new life.

So this is my intention: I will do all I can, stay open and hopeful at every point, and finally surrender my burden to the sky. And surely, surely, out of that, some form of life, even if it is just potash, will mark the spot and something of good will remain to show for it.

CHAPTER TWO

Strength Not to Faint

We had nine months of almost total normalcy. Except for taking medication every day and having a blood check once a month, Laura Lue's life was much as it had been. She made good progress in the third grade, continued her study of violin and ballet, and all kinds of hopes were born in us during these days. Had she been healed? Were the doctors mistaken in their original diagnosis? We hoped so.

But ironically, early Easter Sunday morning she awoke in severe pain. Her eyes began to swell, she hurt all over, and by Monday we were back in Children's Hospital in an acute relapse. Her body had gradually built up an immunity to the medicine that had been helping, and it was no longer effective in holding the disease in check. After ten days of agonizing suffering, a new medicine did take effect, and Laura Lue moved into a second period of remission. The words that follow grew out of the difficult experience of relapse.

Why do you say, O Jacob,
and speak, O Israel,
"My way is hid from the LORD,
and my right is disregarded by my God"?
Have you not known? Have you not heard?
The LORD is the everlasting God, the Creator of the
ends of the earth.
He does not faint or grow weary,
his understanding is unsearchable.
He gives power to the faint,
and to him who has no might he increases strength.
Even youths shall faint and be weary,
and young men shall fall exhausted;
but they who wait for the LORD shall renew their
strength,
they shall mount up with wings like eagles,
they shall run and not be weary,
they shall walk and not faint.

Isaiah 40:27–31

As many of you here already know, the last two weeks have been a stretch of darkness for my family and me. To put the matter more accurately, we have experienced a recurrence of the shadow that first fell across our lives last summer when we learned that our daughter, Laura Lue, had acute leukemia. But then, when the diagnosis was firmed up and treatment was begun, she responded very positively, and as a result we have had over nine months of near-normalcy, what the doctors call "a remission."

Understandably, certain distant hopes developed in our minds. I found myself wondering if perhaps the diagnosis had been a mistaken one, and that she would, after all, go on and live a normal life. Or I pondered whether or not she had been totally healed by God. I had prayed for this many times, and hundreds of other people had done the same thing. I certainly believe such is possible.

But all these fragile creations of my hope began to shatter on, of all days, Easter Sunday. Laura Lue awoke about four o'clock that morning with pains that subsequently led her into the hospital and to the discovery that she had relapsed out of her remission and the mountain was there to be climbed all over again. Of course, this is certainly not the end of the line for us medically and by no means the point of no return so far as ultimate hope is concerned. But there is no denying that it was a disappointment and a further indication as to the nature of the disease and what we can likely expect in the future.

Last summer when all of these problems began, some of you will recall that I came to this pulpit and shared with you out of that first darkness. I did that partly out of my understanding of the nature of the church; namely, that we are a family, bound together as brothers and sisters in Jesus Christ, and therefore what happened to one of us makes a difference to all of us. I shared with you also out of my understanding of my particular role as the pastor of this church. As I see it, part of my job here is to interpret the events of life in terms of their religious implications. It is my belief that God speaks to us and acts on us through the things that happen to us in history. Therefore I could not evade so visible and far-reaching an event in my life. I had to try to tell you what I had learned in that darkness and something of what I thought it meant.

And this morning, for the same reasons, I feel compelled to come to this place and do the same thing. I certainly do not want to exploit this very personal situation; neither do I want to burden you unduly or drag you through something you do not have to face. Yet the fact remains: this is where I am this morning. This crisis has almost totally absorbed my existence for the last two weeks. I have nothing else to share. And more importantly, many of you have let me know that you want to participate with me in this experience.

One of my dearest friends said to me this week: "You know, those of us who have never been through anything like you are experiencing really wonder what it is like. And to be honest, we cannot help asking if one's faith really helps in an extremity such as yours. Does all this talk about God actually make any difference?"

These words did not dismay me a bit, for they reflect the skepticism we all harbor about religious reality. Oh, I know, we go through the motions and affiliate with the institution and even use the words, but when the bottom drops out suddenly as it has for me, we honestly wonder to ourselves what tangible difference faith really makes.

As carefully as I know how this morning, I want to try to deal with that question in terms of personal testimony. In doing so, I want to take the stance of an ordinary human being who is a Christian, and not that of a professional religionist. I realize that by standing in a pulpit and speaking as an ordained minister, many of you will find that hard to accept. You probably think that in order to keep up religious appearances I *have* to say certain things whether they are true or not, but this is not my deliberate stance. I was a human being long before I was a minister, and I made up my mind to be an honest man before I ever came to the conclusion that Christianity was true. Therefore, in approaching this question, I propose to speak, not in deference to some party line, but out of the agony and immediacy of the descent into darkness that has been the last two weeks of my life. I intend to be as honest as I know how to be in bringing this report from the depths.

When the question is raised, "Does faith really make any difference when the bottom drops out?" two presuppositions figure prominently into the answer. One is the kind of expectation one has in a crisis, and the other is the particular vision of God that one takes with oneself into the shadows. The way one reacts to what happens in the depths is going to hinge largely on these factors, so let me be very specific about each one of these in my own situation.

First of all, in the terms of expectations, it seems to me that many people are victimized by false promising. Often, either through their own conjecturing or the zealousness of some preacher or religionist, they have been led to count on certain things happening in a given moment, and when such expectations are not met, disappointment and disillusionment set it.

This very thing happened to C. S. Lewis, a brilliant English scholar who in my judgment was the most notable Christian convert of the twentieth century. From a position of thoroughgoing atheism, he became convinced of the truth of Christianity and emerged as one of the Faith's most insightful interpreters. Lewis, a bachelor up until his middle fifties when he married another adult convert to Christianity, Joy Davidman, had to watch his wife die from cancer only three years after their wedding. In a little book called *A Grief Observed*, which Lewis wrote following that experience, he began by openly acknowledging that at first he was keenly disappointed in what his faith had meant to him in that experience. By the end of the book, however, in his usual perceptive way, he located the problem as one of expectation more than experience. He realized he had taken into that valley certain notions of what ought to happen, and that when those specific things did not occur, his disappointment almost blinded him to the things that were occurring.

In these last two weeks I have been particularly helped by the famous promise in Isaiah 40 that "they who wait upon the Lord shall renew their strength: they shall mount up with wings as eagles; they shall run and not be weary; they shall walk and not faint" (vv. 30–31). Here is the definite promise of divine help, but it is important to notice that such help is described in three different forms, and not all of them ought to be expected in any one situation. This realization is of crucial importance in saving us from false expectations.

For example, there is the promise here that God's strength can take the form of ecstasy, enabling one "to mount up with wings as eagles," to soar away in an atmosphere of sheer exuberance. This is certainly a valid dimension of religious experience, and many times in the past I have known such moments of abandon and celebration and joy. Yet for all its reality, if one were to conclude that this is the only way God give God's strength to humankind, such a one would be vastly disappointed in the kind of darkness through which I have just been walking.

There has been no ecstasy in the last two weeks. How could there have been? Laura Lue suffered more intensely this time than ever before. At one stage both her eyes were swollen shut, and every part of her body seemed to hurt. I stayed with her every night except one while she was in the hospital, and during some of those times she hardly slept for over thirty minutes at a stretch.

In that kind of setting—standing by a bed with a little child moaning and thinking the night would never end—ecstasy is not only inappropriate, it is downright impossible unless one is an insensitive escapist. I realize there are people who tell you that faith can make everything easy and who claim that any time a person prays, that one is caught up in light and soars above problems until they appear small and inconsequential. But I don't believe such words! There are moments in the depths of human suffering when the soaring of ecstasy would be out of touch with reality, and if this is one's only form of expectation—

the only shape of God's strength one can acknowledge—one is sure to feel betrayed and forsaken in the darkness. God does not come in this way to every situation.

A second way that God's help is described in Isaiah is in terms of strength for activism—"they shall run and not be weary." Here, too, is another valid shape of religious experience—the inspiration to do a job or to solve a problem or get on with some task. Now this is something I am familiar with experientially, for my faith has often motivated me and empowered me to get busy with some project and "to work while it is yet day, for the night cometh when no one can work." But once again, this is not the *only* way we experience God. If it were, then the depths would still be a place of disappointment, for more often than not, there is really nothing one can do.

That is the way it was for me there by Laura Lue's bed in the night. If I had no occasion to soar in ecstasy, neither did I have any room to run in activism. We were doing everything we knew to do—leaving no stone unturned, no avenue untried—and still she lay there crying and the problem persisted. If I had been the kind of person who looked to God for "answers" or programs of activity that had to lead to concrete solutions, I would once again have been frustrated. There was no way to attack this problem by force, no solution of activism or energy. There was simply no room "to run and not be weary."

Fortunately, there is one other form that the promise of God's strength takes: "They shall walk and not faint." Now I am sure that to those looking for the spectacular, this may sound insignificant indeed. Who wants to be slowed to a walk, to creep along inch by inch, just barely above the threshold of consciousness and not fainting? That may not sound like much of a religious experience, but believe me, in the kind of darkness where I have been, it is the only form of the promise that fits the situation. When there is no occasion to soar and no place to run, and all you can do is edge along step by step, to hear of a Help that will enable you "to walk and not faint" is good news indeed. It not only corresponds to the limits of the situation, it also speaks to the point of greatest difficulty; namely, of being able just "to hang in there," to endure, to be patient, and not to give down one way or the other.

The hardest thing of all for me in the last two weeks has been my helplessness in the face of Laura Lue's suffering. If only there had been something I could have done to change things tangibly, it would have been easier—but there was not. All I could do was stand there by the bed and give her a sip of water now and then and rub her and reassure her, and it seemed like so little in the face of such an immensity. The very tedium of it, the slow endless pace of the hours of the night—at times it almost got unbearable. In that kind of boxed-in setting, the challenge of being able "to walk and not faint" becomes the most demanding challenge of all. Some people feel the sequence of this Isaiah passage is all turned around and that the highest form of God's help ought to be the soaring of ecstasy. They say it should read, "First you walk, then you run, and finally you mount up with wings as an eagle." But I think the writer knew what he was doing when he set down the promises as he did, for in the dark stretches of life, the most difficult discipline of all is not that of soaring or even of running. It consists of "keeping on keeping on" when events have slowed you to a walk, when it seems that in spite of everything you are going to crumple under the load and faint away.

Joseph Pieper has observed that the two classic forms that temptation takes are presumption and despair. He describes the first of these as getting so frustrated with God that one takes things into one's own hands and explodes in some fit of rage. The other is to give up altogether and dissolve into despair.

I experienced both of these forms of temptation in a most acute way. My presumptive temptation was to get angry and rebellious toward God and thus "overheat" my spirit. As I watched my little daughter suffer, I could see no reason or purpose in what was happening to her. The flow of events did not seem to be going in any meaningful direction, and I had my moments when I understood how a person could raise one's fist to heaven and curse God. At times I was not far from looking up and shouting: "Just what on earth do You think that You are doing in all of this anyway?" At other times the temptation to despair was very strong, when I felt like saying: "I quit. I give up. I can't stand it any longer. Stop the world. I want to get off."

Yes, both of these temptations loomed large on the horizon as I stood there helpless in the darkness, but I am here to report that I did not succumb to either one. Why? Because down there at the bottom—this promise of Isaiah came true! I was given the gift of patience, the gift of enduring. I was given the strength "to walk and not faint."

The least of gifts, you say? Maybe so, from one standpoint, yet in another way, it was the most appropriate of all the gifts, the one thing most needful in that situation. And because I was willing to settle for it—so little and yet so much, I can say honestly: my faith did make a difference when the bottom dropped out. It kept me from giving up!

But I repeat: this happened because my expectations were not distorted. If I had said: "It has got to be ecstasy or some solution of activism if it is God's help," then I would have been sorely disappointed, for all I got at the bottom there was strength to walk and not faint, just enough power "to hang in there" and not give up. And this was enough for me, and because I was not demanding or expecting a lot more, my faith did make a difference—in fact, I would have to say: the crucial difference!

Expectation, then, was one of the keys in enabling me to give an affirmative answer to this question. The other factor was the vision of God I took with me into this situation. I think it needs to be said that long before Laura Lue's sickness came upon us, I had struggled with the question of who God was and what God was like. I have shared at other times with you how I went through a long period of doubt and agnosticism, until finally, by God's grace and because of my openness, the Mystery of Godness made God's self known in the history of Israel and the face of Jesus Christ. Therefore, I already had some conviction, born in the light, that I was able to carry into the darkness and use as a frame of understanding. What would have happened in this moment had I never struggled before with Ultimate Reality or faced the God-question I will never know. One does not sow and reap in the same day, and, quite honestly, I must acknowledge that if this tragedy were my only conscious experience with God, I probably would not have come out where I did.

My situation is like that of the exiles to whom this passage in Isaiah is addressed. They, too, had fallen on hard times and were separated from all their hopes and dreams, and the prophet bids them remember what they have learned of God in better times. "Have you not known?" he asks. "Have you not heard what God is like?" Then he begins to paint with broad strokes what the God of Israel had shown God's self to be. God is "the everlasting Lord," "the Creator of the ends of the earth"; that is, God is present with them, lovingly and powerfully in their situation. God is mysterious; that is, "God's understanding is unsearchable." What God does is not always immediately evident to human eyes. God is also inexhaustible in energy: "God does not faint or grow weary." And best of all, it is God's nature "to give power to the faint, and to those who have no might, God increases strength."

Such a vision of God stands in marked contrast to the pagan images of divinity outside biblical religion. In their thinking, the gods were not present as a loving Creator, but distant and indifferent, off in another realm. Pagan gods did not act purposefully in history, and most of all they did not care for weak people. Yet the God of Israel was just the opposite. God was like a Shepherd who cared tenderly for all his flock. This meant that the weak and the stragglers got extra attention. And in the great procession of humanity, who had sunk any lower or straggled any farther behind than the ragtag group of slaves down in Egypt? Yet it was to them that the great Shepherd-God turned his attention. And in the way God brought them forth, like a shepherd carrying lambs on his bosom, God made known to the world what God was really like—the Everlasting Lord, the Creator of the ends of earth, the One whose understanding is unsearchable, "who fainteth not, neither is weary, and whose nature it is to give power to the faint."

It is this vision of God, already made known to them in their history, that the exiles were called to remember and then to apply to their situation. And when they did, it was promised that their strength would be renewed. This is exactly what I did during those days of darkness down at Children's Hospital. I remembered the God who had made God's self known to me in the light, and I interpreted that situation there in relation to this understanding. This means that I believed God was present there with us, involved in every moment of suffering and pain. I believed God was there as Mystery, that God's ways were too big for me to get my mind around in understanding. I believed God was there as inexhaustible energy, not weary and weak as we were.

Therefore, I was not disappointed. At the bottom of the darkness, my faith truly did make a difference. Why? Partly because I did not erect false expectations; I let God be God and give me what God willed to give and what was appropriate. And also because long before, I had come to see God as a Shepherd-God—the One whose nature it is to give power to the faint; therefore I was open at the point of helplessness. And believe me, my friends, God came and "did God's thing" for me. God gave power to me, the faint; for me, the one who had no might, God increased my strength.

Well, that is how it was, and here I am this morning— sad, brokenhearted, still bearing in my spirit the wounds of the darkness. I confess to you honestly that I have no wings with which to fly or even any legs on which to run—but listen, by the grace of God, *I am still on my feet!* I have not fainted yet. I have not exploded in the anger of presumption, nor have I keeled over into the paralysis of despair. All I am doing is walking and not fainting, hanging in there, enduring with patience what I cannot change but have to bear.

This may not sound like much to you, but to me it is the most appropriate and most needful of all the gifts. My faith has been the difference in the last two weeks; it has given me the gift of patience, the gift of endurance, the strength to walk and not faint. And I am here to give thanks to God for that!

And who knows, if I am willing to accept this gift, and just hang in there and not cop out, maybe the day will come that Laura Lue and I can run again and not be weary, and that we may even soar some day, and rise up with wings as eagles! But until then—to walk and not faint, that is enough. O God, that is enough!

CHAPTER THREE

Life Is Gift

The second medicine was as effective as the first, but for a shorter time span. In August, at the end of our family vacation, several things began to happen and we were never able to maintain another period of remission, although at least four other medicines were tried. Laura Lue attended school only a few scattered days that fall. Our life revolved around intermittent periods of hospitalization and unnumbered trips to the outpatient clinic and emergency room of Children's Hospital. Toward the end, the treatments became almost impossible, and created the added strain of trying to decide what to continue and what to forgo.

We had a memorable Christmas day, which Laura Lue anticipated greatly and planned for carefully. But when that was over, her life processes began to wane. Just two weeks later on a Saturday evening, with the snow falling softly outside the window, Laura Lue died in her own bed, in her own room.

It was a month before I attempted to preach again, and these are the words that broke that prolonged silence.

After these things God tested Abraham, and said to him,
"Abraham!" And he said, "Here am I." He said, "Take your son,
your only son Isaac, whom you love, and go to the land of
Moriah, and offer him there as a burnt offering upon one of the
mountains of which I shall tell you." So Abraham rose early in
the morning, saddled his ass, and took two of his young men
with him, and his son Isaac; and he cut the wood for the burnt
offering, and arose and went to the place of which God had told
him. On the third day Abraham lifted up his eyes and saw the
place afar off. Then Abraham said to his young men, "Stay here
with the ass; I and the lad will go yonder and worship, and
come again to you." And Abraham took the wood of the burnt
offering, and laid it on Isaac his son; and he took in his hand
the fire and the knife. So they went both of them together. And
Isaac said to his father Abraham, "My father!" And he said,
"Here am I, my son." He said, "Behold, the fire and the wood;
but where is the lamb for a burnt offering ?" Abraham said,
"God will provide himself the lamb for a burnt offering, my
son." So they went both of them together.

When they came to the place of which God had told him,
Abraham built an altar there, and laid the wood in order, and

bound Isaac his son, and laid him on the altar, upon the wood. Then Abraham put forth his hand, and took the knife to slay his son. But the angel of the LORD called to him from heaven, and said "Abraham, Abraham!" And he said, "Here am!" He said, "Do not lay your hand on the lad or do anything to him; for now I know that you fear God, seeing you have not withheld your son, your only son, from me." And Abraham lifted up his eyes and looked, and behold, behind him was a ram, caught in a thicket by his horns; and Abraham went and took the ram, and offered it up as a burnt offering instead of his son. So Abraham called the name of that place The LORD will Provide; as it is said to this day, "On the mount of the LORD it shall be provided."

Genesis 22:1–14

For the last eighteen months now, this particular episode out of the life of Abraham has held a great fascination for me. As you might suspect, I can identify in large measure with much that took place there. For example, I know something of the overwhelming shock that Abraham must have experienced when he realized one night that God was demanding his son of him. I found myself engulfed in a torrent of emotions identical to that a year ago last June when I first heard the word "leukemia" spoken about my child. There is no way to describe the mixture of horror and bitterness and terror and fear that churns up within one at the advent of such a realization.

I can also identify with the way Abraham proceeded to respond to this eventuality. As I see him slowly setting out on this journey he had no desire to take, I can almost sense the double agenda that was going on within him. Though intellectually he realized that the worst could very well happen, he does not try to run away but sets his face steadfastly for Moriah. Yet emotionally there is a hope within him that something will intervene even at the last moment to reverse the process.

Abraham gives expression to this residual hope there at the foot of the mountain when little Isaac asks about the lamb for the sacrifice, and I know exactly how he felt. I, too, have lived these last eighteen months with the same double agenda. Facing up with my mind to the fact that Laura Lue's situation was very serious, I did everything in my power to cope with it realistically. But at the feeling level, I had abounding hope. In fact, I did not realize just how hopeful I really was until that Saturday afternoon as I knelt by her bed and saw her stop breathing. You may find this incredible, but I was the most shocked person in all the world at that moment. You see, deep down, I did not believe she was going to die. In spite of all my mind told me, I found myself clinging to the hope that any day a cure would be found, or that God would see fit to heal her miraculously. I certainly did not demand this of God or feel that God owed it to us. I simply believed that what had happened for Abraham would happen for us, and that even if it came at the last moment, the knife would be stayed.

But, of course, that is not what happened four weeks ago last Saturday, and I am still in the process of trying to take in what did in fact occur. It is at this point that Abraham's experience and my own break off in different directions. He got to go down the mountain with his child by his side, arid, oh, how his heart must have burst with joy at having come through so much so well.

But my situation is different. Here I am, left alone on that mountain, with my child and not a ram there on the altar, and the question is: how on earth do I get down and move back to the normalcy of life again? I cannot learn from Abraham, lucky man that he is. I am left to grope through the darkness by myself, and to ask: "Where do I go from here? Is there a road out, and if so, which one?"

Let me hasten to admit that I am really in no position to speak with any finality to such a question this morning, for I am still much in shock, much at sea, very much broken and by no means fully healed. What I have to share is of a highly provisional character, for as of now the light is very dim. However, if you will accept it as such, I do feel I have made a few discoveries in these last four weeks that may be of worth to some of you. To be very specific, now that I have looked down three alternative roads that seem to lead out of this darkness, I must report that two of them appear to be dead ends, while a third holds real promise.

The first of these routes comes highly recommended, and I would label it "the road of unquestioning resignation." If I have been told once, I have been told a hundred times: "We must not question God. We must not try to understand. We have no right to ask or to inquire into the ways of God with humankind. The way out is to submit. We must silently and totally surrender. We must accept what God does without a word or a murmur."

Now there is both ancient and practical wisdom in this approach to deep sorrow, and in one sense it is utterly realistic, for if I have learned anything in all of this, it is just how weak and ineffectual we humans are against the immensities of life and death. Since I was powerless a month ago to do anything to avert this agony, why bother now to try to struggle with it? I repeat, there is a wisdom of sorts down this road of unquestioning resignation. The only trouble is, it is not a Christian wisdom, and in fact it is a denial of the heart of our faith. I have been frankly dismayed at how many deeply devoted Christians have recommended this way to me, and I have wondered to myself: "Don't they realize what such an approach implies about the whole of existence?"

To put it bluntly, this sort of silent submission undermines the most precious dimension of our existence; namely, our personhood. It reduces all of life to a mechanical power transaction. To be sure, a leaf submits to the wind without saying a word, and a rock allows the flood water to do whatever it pleases without murmur, but are these appropriate analogies for a relationship between God and human beings?

According to the Bible, they are not, for in this document the mystery of Godness is depicted as involving more than brute force. The One who moves through these pages is by nature a Being of love, "a Father who pitieth his children" rather than a Force who knocks about a lot of helpless objects. And of course, words and questions and dialogue back and forth are at the heart of the way that persons—especially parents and children—ought to relate.

Where, then, did we Christians ever get the notion that we must not question God or that we have no right to pour out our souls to God and ask, Why? Did not Job in the Old Testament cry out to God in the midst of his agony and attempt to interrogate the Almighty? Did not Jesus himself agonize with God in Gethsemane, telling God how he felt and what he wanted, and then cry out from the Cross: "My God, My God! Why? Why have you forsaken me?" Would the verse "Ask and it shall be given you, seek and you shall find, knock and it shall be opened unto you" ever have appeared in Holy Scripture if unquestioning acquiescence had been the way to meet tragedy?

I, for one, see nothing but a dead end down this road of silent resignation, for it is one of those medicines that cures at the expense of killing the organism it is supposed to heal. After all, my questions in the face of this event are a real part of me just now, and to deny them or to suppress them by bowing mechanically to a superior Force is an affront not only to God and to my own nature, but also to the kind of relation we are supposed to have.

There is more honest faith in an act of questioning than in the act of silent submission, for implicit in the very asking is the faith that some light can be given. This is why I found such help in a letter I received from Dr. Carlyle Marney just before Laura Lue died. He admitted that he had no word for the suffering of the innocent and never had, but he said: "I fall back on the notion that God has a lot to give an account for."

Now, to be honest, no one had ever said anything like that to me before, and at first, it was a little shocking, but the more I thought about it, the truer it seemed in light of the faith of the Bible. At no point in its teaching is there ever an indication that God wants us to remain like rocks or even little infants in our relationship to God. God wants us to become mature sons and daughters, which means that God holds us responsible for our actions and expects us to hold him responsible for his!

I do not believe God wants me to hold in these questions that burn in my heart and soul—questions like: "Why is there leukemia? Why are children of promise cut down at the age of ten? Why did You let Laura Lue suffer so excruciatingly and then let her die?" I am really honoring God when I come clean and say, "You owe me an explanation." For, you see, I believe God will be able to give such an accounting when all the facts are in, and until then, it is valid to ask.

It is not rebelliousness, then, but faith that keeps me from finding any promise down the road of unquestioning resignation. This approach is closer to pagan Stoicism than Christian humility. I have no choice but to submit to this event of death. Still, the questions remain, and I believe I honor God by continuing to ask and seek and knock rather than resigning myself like a leaf or a rock.

Having said that, however, I need to hasten on to identify a second dead-end route, lest I badly confuse you. It is what I would call "the road of total intellectual understanding," the way of explaining everything completely or tying up all the loose ends in a tidy answer. To be sure, I have just said that I believe some day God will be able to give account for what God has done and show how it all fits together, but that eschaton is not now. Accordingly, any attempt at this moment to absolutize or to find an answer that will account for all the evidence will either end in failure or be a real distortion of reality.

I perhaps need to confess to you that at times in the last few months I have been tempted to conclude that this whole existence of ours is utterly absurd. More than once I looked radical doubt full in the face and honestly wondered if all our talk about love and purpose and a fatherly

God were not simply a veil of fantasy that we pathetic humans had projected against the void. For you see, in light of the evidence closest at hand, to have absolutized at all would have been to conclude that all was absurd and there was no Ultimate Purpose. There were the times, for example, when Laura Lue was hurting so intensely that she had to bite on a rag and used to beg me to pray to God to take away that awful pain. I would kneel down beside her bed and pray with all the faith and conviction of my soul, and nothing would happen except the pain continuing to rage on. Or again, that same negative conclusion was tempting when she asked me in the dark of the night: "When will this leukemia go away?" I answered: "I don't know, darling, but we are doing everything we know to make that happen." Then she said: "Have you asked God when it will go away?" And I said: "Yes, you have heard me pray to him many times." But she persisted: "What did God say? When did God say it would go away?" And I had to admit God had not said a word! I had done a lot of talking and praying and pleading, but the response of the heavens had been one of silence.

And although in moments like that I was tempted to absolutize about life and arrange all existence around one explaining principle, clearer moments made me realize that such simplicity would not correspond to reality. For you see, alongside the utter absurdity of what was happening to this little girl were countless other experiences that were full of love and purpose and meaning. From people in the clinic and at the hospital, from unnumbered hosts of you in the church and the community, came evidences of goodness that were anything but absurd. And I realized if I were going to judge it all fairly, this data had to be balanced in with equal weight alongside all the darkness.

I was reminded of a conclusion I came to a long time ago that was you do not solve all the intellectual problems by deciding that everything is absurd. To be sure, it is hard to account for evil on the assumption that God is all-good and all-powerful, but if you do away with that assumption and go to the other extreme, you are then left with the problem of how to account for all the goodness and purpose that most assuredly also exist. This leads me to conclude that expecting to find one total explanation or answer to this situation is futile.

Never has the stark paradox of real darkness alongside real light been more apparent to me than in the last days, which means I shall continue to ask questions, but not expect, in history at least, to find any complete answer. George Buttrick is right in saying that life is essentially a series of events to be borne and lived through rather than intellectual riddles to be played with and solved. Courage is worth ten times more than any answer that claims to be total. We cannot absolutize in such a way that either the darkness swallows up the light or the light the darkness. To do so would be untrue to our human condition that "knows in part" and does all its seeing "as through a glass darkly."

For me, at least, the roads called unquestioning resignation and total understanding hold no promise of leading out of the darkness where I lost my child. But remember, I said in the beginning there was a third way, and what little I have learned of it I now want to share.

I call this one "the road of gratitude," and interestingly enough, it is basic to the story of Abraham and Isaac that serves as our text. Years ago, when I first started taking the Bible seriously, this whole episode used to bother me a good deal. What kind of jealous God is it, I wondered, who would demand a man's child as a sign of devotion? As I moved more deeply into the biblical revelation, however, I came to realize that the point at issue in this event was not that at all. What God was trying to teach Abraham here and throughout his whole existence was the basic understanding that life is a gift—pure, simple, sheer gift—and that we here on earth are to relate to it accordingly.

The promise that came originally to Abraham from God was literally "out of the blue." Just as he had not been in on the creation of the world or his own birth, so Abraham had done nothing to earn the right of having a land of his own or descendants more numerous than the stars. Such a promise came as pure gift from God. Abraham was called on to receive it, to participate in it fully and joyfully, to handle it with the open hands of gratitude.

And this, of course, is an image of how human beings were meant to relate to existence itself. Life, too, is a gift, and it is to be received and participated in and handled with gratitude.

But right here is the problem. God had to start all over again with Abraham, because humankind had lost this view of life and instead had tried to earn life by the ardors of legalism or to possess it totally as if it belonged to them alone. All these mistaken relations, of course, served only to curdle life and make of it a crushing burden or a prison of anxiety.

The whole point in the Abraham saga lies in God's effort to restore human beings to a right vision of life and a right relationship to it. Only when life is seen as a gift and received with the open hands of gratitude is it the joy God meant for it to be. And these were the truths God was seeking to emphasize as God waited so long to send Isaac and then asked for him back. Did Abraham realize that all was gift, and not something to be earned or to be possessed; but received, participated in, held freely in gratefulness? This is the most helpful perspective I have found in the last weeks, and of all the roads to travel, it offered the best promise of being a way out and a way through.

Something that happened to me years ago may help you to understand what I mean. When World War II started, my family did not have a washing machine. With gas rationed and the laundry several miles away, keeping our clothes clean became an intensely practical problem.

One of my father's younger business associates was drafted and his wife prepared to go with him, and we offered to let them store their furniture in our basement. Quite unexpectedly, they suggested that we use their washing machine while they were gone. "It would be better for it to be running," they said, "than sitting up rusting." So this is what we did, and it helped us a great deal.

Since I used to help with the washing, across the years I developed quite an affectionate relation for that old green Bendix. But eventually the war ended, and our friends returned, and in the meantime I had forgotten how the machine had come to be in our basement in the first place. When they came and took it, I was terribly upset and I said so quite openly.

But my mother, being the wise woman she is, sat me down and put things in perspective. She said, "Wait a minute, son. You must remember, that machine never belonged to us in the first place. That we ever got to use it at all was a gift. So, instead of being mad at its being taken away, let's use this occasion to be grateful that we ever had it at all."

Here, in a nutshell, is what, it means to understand something as a gift and to handle it with gratitude, a perspective biblical religion puts around all of life. And I am here to testify that this seems to me to be the best way down from the Mountain of Loss. I do not mean to say that such a perspective makes things easy, for it does not. But at least it makes things bearable when I remember that Laura Lue was gift, pure and simple, something I neither earned nor deserved nor had a right to. And when I remember that the appropriate response to a gift, even when it is taken away, is gratitude, then I am better able to try and thank God that I was ever given her in the first place.

Even though it is very, very hard, I am doing my best to learn this discipline now. Everywhere I turn I am surrounded by reminders of her—things we did together, things she said, things she loved. And in the presence of these reminders, I have two alternatives. I can dwell on the fact that she has been taken away, and dissolve in remorse that all of this is gone forever. Or, focusing on the wonder that she was ever given at all, I can resolve to be grateful that we shared life, even for an all-too-short ten years. There are only two choices here, but believe me, the best way out for me is the way of gratitude. The way of remorse does not alter the stark reality one whit and only makes matters worse. The way of gratitude does not alleviate the pain, but it somehow puts some light around the darkness and creates strength to begin to move on.

Now, having gone full circle, I come back to caution you not to look to me this morning as an authority on how to deal with grief. Rather, I need you to help me on down the way, and this is how: do not counsel me not to question, and do not attempt to give me any total answers. Neither one of those ways will work for me. The greatest thing you can do is to remind me that life is gift—every particle of it, and that the way to handle a gift is to be grateful. You can really help me if you will never let me forget this fact, just as I hope maybe I have helped some of you this morning by reminding you of the same thing. As I see it now, the best way out of darkness is the way of gratitude. Will you join me in trying to learn how to travel that way?

CHAPTER FOUR

Learning to Handle Grief

It has been three and one half years now since Laura Lue died, and we have moved to another city and a new church. I have had occasion to reflect at more distance on the grief process, and delivered this sermon on the Sunday of Memorial Day weekend in 1973. The various stages described here accurately reflect my pilgrimage, and these words are added to set the process of bereavement in larger perspective.

There was a man in the land of Uz, whose name was Job; and that man was blameless and upright, one who feared God, and turned away from evil. . . . Now there was a day when his sons and daughters were eating and drinking wine in their eldest brother's house; and there came a messenger to Job, and said, "The oxen were plowing and the asses feeding beside them; and the Sabeans fell upon them and took them, and slew the servants with the edge of the sword; and I alone have escaped to tell you." While he was yet speaking, there came another, and said, "The fire of God fell from heaven and burned up the sheep and the servants, and consumed them; and I alone have escaped to tell you." While he was yet speaking, there came another, and said, "The Chaldeans formed three companies, and made a raid upon the camels and took them, and slew the servants with the edge of the sword; and I alone have escaped to tell you." While he was yet speaking, there came another, and said, "Your sons and daughters were eating and drinking wine in their eldest brother's house; and behold, a great wind came across the wilderness, and struck the four corners of the house, and it fell upon the young people, and they are dead; and I alone have escaped to tell you."

Then Job arose, and rent his robe, and shaved his head, and fell upon the ground, and worshiped. . . .

So Satan went forth from the presence of the LORD, and afflicted Job with loathsome sores from the sole of his foot to the crown of his head. And he took a potsherd with which to scrape himself; and sat among the ashes.

Then his wife said to him, "Do you still hold fast your integrity? Curse God, and die."

But he said to her, "You speak as one of the foolish women would speak. Shall we receive good at the hand of God, and shall we not receive evil?" In all this Job did not sin with his lips. . . .

After this Job opened his mouth and cursed the day of his birth. And Job said: "Let the day perish wherein I was born, and the night which said, 'A man-child is conceived.' . . .

"Why is light given to him that is in misery, and life to the bitter in soul, who long for death, but it comes not, and dig for it more than for hid treasures; who rejoice exceedingly, and are glad, when they find the grave? Why is light given to a man whose way is hid, whom God has hedged in?" . . .

"Oh that I were as in the months of old, as in the days when God watched over me; when his lamp shone upon my head, and by his light I walked through darkness; as I was in my autumn

72

days, when the friendship of God was upon my tent; when the Almighty was yet with me, when my children were about me; when my steps were washed with milk, and the rock poured out for me streams of oil!" . . . Then Job answered the LORD: "I know that thou canst do all things, and that no purpose of thine can be thwarted. 'Who is this that hides counsel without knowledge?' Therefore I have uttered what I did not understand, things too wonderful for me, which I did not know. 'Hear, and I will speak; I will question you, and you declare to me.' I had heard of thee by the hearing of the ear, but now my eye sees thee; therefore I despise myself, and repent in dust and ashes." . . .

And the LORD restored the fortunes of Job, when he had prayed for his friends; and the LORD gave Job twice as much as he had before.

Job 1:1, 13–20; 2:7–10; 3:1–3, 20–23; 29:2–6; 42:1–6, 10

The familiar words used to describe the suffering servant in the fifty-third chapter of Isaiah could just as readily be said of Job: "He was a person of sorrows, acquainted with grief." Actually, they are descriptive of us all, of every person who has lived very long on this earth. It is true that many of us think of grief only in relation to bereavement and death, and this is the most intense form of the experience, of course. But as a matter of fact, any time we lose something that is of value to us, the feelings we experience are feelings of grief.

Learning to handle these in a healthy way—learning how to lose, so to speak—is one of life's most important challenges. It can hardly be begun too soon. As parents we have the instinct to shield our children in this area. I have known people who think that by not letting their little ones go to a funeral home or a funeral service, they are sparing them exposure to grief. But this is really not the case, for as soon as child is old enough to love something that can be lost, that one is a candidate to become "a person of sorrows, acquainted with grief." Very few get very far without experiencing loss in some way.

I remember vividly when I was first initiated into the fraternity of the sorrowing. I must have been about four. An uncle of mine had just given me my first puppy, a fat butterball of brown and white fur named Jiggs. He was the delight of my life and my constant companion. One morning I went out in the backyard to feed him and, having romped awhile, started back into the house. Unbeknown to me, Jiggs tried to follow. Quite by accident the screen door slammed on him and happened to catch his neck in just the place to break it. There before my eyes he had a convulsion and died. To this very moment I can still recall the feeling of horror and unbelief that swept over me at that sight, and for hours afterward I cried uncontrollably. I was only four, but already I was "acquainted with grief."

I had similar emotions, although not as traumatic, when the father of my best friend in the third grade got transferred to another city and suddenly George Hunt was gone out of my life forever. And then there was the time I inadvertently lost a ring that my grandmother Claypool had given me before she died, and I felt real emptiness in being without that beloved object. You see, before I was very old at all, in relation to the animals and the people and the objects of my life, I was "a person of sorrow, acquainted with grief."

The truth is—for every one of us—that there is no way to avoid the trauma of loss if we love even a little. This is what makes the task of learning to handle grief so important. The patterns we develop early in relation to our "little griefs" will affect how we react when the trauma of bereavement comes upon us. No one sows and reaps in the same day, so learning how to lose creatively is not something we can afford to postpone. On this Memorial Day Sunday, therefore, when it is natural for us to think of the ultimate form of grief, I would like for us to look at the whole process and see how we can come to understand it better and thus be more able to work our way through it.

As a means to that end, I would like for us to use one of the great documents of the Old Testament, the Book of Job. The light of this magnificent dramatic poem shines in many directions, but this morning let us approach it from only one angle—the management of grief—and study how one person coped with the experience that is common to us all.

If you are familiar with the story, you know that at the beginning Job was a wealthy man in every sense of that term. He had a great deal of property, a large and happy family, and enjoyed the universal esteem of his peers. In the unfolding of the drama, however, suddenly and systematically every one of these objects of value was taken away from him. He lost his possessions through conquest and calamity. His children were all killed when a tornado struck the house where they were eating. And finally his own health was taken from him and he was left covered with boils, utterly alone and bereft of everything he had once possessed. Here in a most acute form is the human experience of loss. Let us learn what we can by noting exactly how Job coped with this situation. There are several discernible stages in Job's movement through this "valley of the shadow of grief," all of which I want us to trace. The pattern is similar to every person's experience.

Job's first reaction was one of numbed shock. When his three friends came to console him, they sat for seven days and nights in utter silence, for Job's losses had been so great that at first they could hardly be taken in.

Nearly everyone has this initial reaction to the trauma of loss. There is so much within us that does not want to accept the actuality of it that our unconscious works against our doing so. Thus it is not at all uncommon for a person under the initial impact of loss to be in something of a daze or walking around as if in a dream.

But this state of numbed awareness, which is so merciful at first, does not last forever. Sooner or later the awesome reality of what has occurred begins to dawn on the griever. And this is what we see happening to Job as he moves into his second state of coping.

At this point everything looks utterly hopeless to him. He curses the day he was born and even the night he was conceived, and he makes it clear that if he could die immediately it would suit him fine. Meaning totally collapses for him. As the full extent of what he has lost begins to dawn upon Job, he sees no future left for him. So much of his familiar world has died, part of him has died as well, and his first impulse is to say: "I wish I had never been born at all into this vale of tears. Now that I am here, please stop the world; I want to get off!" Anyone who has ever experienced profound loss is totally familiar with such sentiments. When it first begins to settle in how utterly life has been altered, there appears to be no hope, no reason for going on, no possibility that there could ever again be anything worth living for. Clouds of despair engulf the horizon, and the impulse to do what Job's wife suggested— to regard the whole experience as a total curse and give up—seems to be the most appropriate response.

But familiar and understandable as these feelings may be, as a rule they too do not persist forever. Suicide is not the answer, one begins to realize; somehow one must go on.

Job goes through just this thought process in stage number three. He begins to come to terms with reality, and quite predictably he turns instinctively to the most appealing aspect of it: his memories of the past. For a while he goes back in time and revels in nostalgia. He remembers "the good old days" when his children were with him and his possessions were intact and he had the esteem of the community. The first positive thoughts that come to him in his depression have to do with how good life used to be. But this reaction, though very common, often activates a sense of guilt also, in which one says: "I should have been more grateful for those good days. If I had only realized then how blessed I was, I would have behaved differently. I would have said more loving things to my family. I would not have done the cruel things that I did." In other words, because the experience of loss makes one realize anew the value of what used to be, it drives one back into the past with great emotion, as Job found.

In the grieving process, this is a crucial moment. The temptation to turn away from reality and to live only in the world of fantasy is very great once the values of the past are fully appreciated. Yet to make this into a way of life is tragic indeed. Just as fantasy images of food cannot nourish the body, so the realm of memories, precious and pleasant as they are, cannot provide us the support that is needed for the living of life. For Job, it was fortunate that his "sentimental journey" into the past did not end in his staying there. Rather, he returned to the present and to a more realistic assessment of where he was and what he had lost, and thus marked his passage into stage number four.

Stage four could well be characterized as the place of anger and resentment, for as Job reflected on his loss, he began to look for someone to blame. In my judgment, these feelings in Job were intensified because of what his three so-called "comforters" were trying to do. Living in a day of simple equations, they were intent on finding an explanation for Job's troubles. Prosperity meant one was righteous; suffering meant one was sinning. Under the guise of consoling, they attempted to blame Job and make him confess some hidden sin in his life that could account for all this calamity. Job reacted defensively to these accusations. Although he did not claim to be sinless, he could not accept their simplistic reasoning. Instead, he took the stance of blaming God and saying that the whole scheme of things that lets such events occur was unjust.

I think there is an important lesson for us to learn here about how to help others in the grieving process: it is always futile and unproductive to try to explain tragedy in some comprehensive way. Saying piously that a loss is "the will of God" does not solve anything and may even create a sense of anger in the person who has been hurt. The calamities of life are all deeply mysterious and the more we try to "explain" them to each other and fix the blame and responsibility here or there, the further we get from the truth. Job's friends, because of their misguided intellectualizing, actually stimulated in him a seething resentment against God and the whole universe. Admittedly, he might have come to this position on his own, but there is no doubt he was driven forward by his friends.

The basic issue in grief is never a rational explanation anyway. What matters is the nature of life itself and the One who gives it. Not until Job got to that level—to having it out with the Ultimate One—did healing begin to flow for him. Stage five, the climactic stage, came when Job, the one who was made, stood face to face with the One who did the making.

Two things that radically altered Job's situation emerged out of this encounter, and they proved to be the catalyst that enabled Job to move through his grief back to wholeness. One was a new understanding of the past, and the other was a fresh vision of the future. Let us look at them both.

The first thing God did was to call into question the "justice-injustice" approach to the mystery of life. God began by asking Job where he had been when the whole drama of creation had begun. What had he done to create his own life, or to call the universe into being, or to make possible the existence of his possessions or his children or his health? In other words, God was reminding Job that the things he had become so indignant about losing actually did not belong to him in the first place. They were gifts—gifts beyond his deserving, graciously given him by Another, and thus not to be possessed or held onto as if they were his. To be angry because a gift has been taken away is to miss the whole point of life. That we ever have the things we cherish is more than we deserve. Gratitude and humility rather than resentment should characterize our handling of the objects of life. This important lesson is one all of us need to learn. Hugh Prather states the point well in a little piece he wrote during an illness his wife suffered. As she slept by his side, he mused:

> She may die before morning. But I have been with her for four years. Four years. There is no way I could feel cheated if I didn't have her for another day. I didn't deserve her for one minute, God knows.
>
> And I may die before morning.
> What I must do is die now. I must accept the justice of death and the injustice of life. I have lived a good life— longer than many, better than most. Tony died when he was twenty. I have had thirty-two years. I couldn't ask for another day. What did I do to deserve birth? It was a gift.

I am me—that is a miracle. I had no right to a single minute. Some are given a single hour. And yet I have had thirty-two years.

Few can choose when they will die. I choose to accept death now. As of this moment I give up my "right" to live. And I give up my "right" to her life.

But it's morning. I have been given another day. Another day to hear and read and smell and walk and love and glory. I am alive for another day.*

This is exactly what God said to Job out of the whirlwind. He reminded him where all the treasures of the past had come from and what they were—gifts beyond his deserving. And it was this new understanding of the past, this realization that nothing really belongs to us in the sense that we have a right to it, that gave Job a sense of perspective about his losses and started him on the upward swing of healing.

The other insight that came to Job was a fresh vision of the future. God made it clear that he had not been totally

---

*From Hugh Prather, *Notes to Myself: My Struggle to Become a Person* (Moab, Utah: Real People Press, 1970).

defeated by the events of the past but was still capable of giving meaning to Job's life. In other words, apart from all appearances, Job still had a future in God, for God had a future for Job.

No one ever moves out of the shadows of grief apart from some form of this hope. Myron Madden is right when he says, "The essence of despair is relegating God solely to the past." And what is nostalgia if it is not the fear that God cannot do as well in the future as God has done in the past?

What Job discovered in his encounter with God was that goodness and mercy can be counted on to follow us "all the days of our life," just as the Psalmist said. He who has given us the good gifts of the past can be depended on to continue to give meaning to our lives. Our challenge, then is to become flexible enough and trusting enough to let this happen.

Part of the problem in our grieving is idolatry; that is, making gods out of certain people or objects and then refusing either to let them go or to receive other gifts from God. We say rebelliously: "If I can't keep on having this or that gift, I don't want anything at all."

The other part of the problem is not trusting the creativity of God enough to believe God can give us new things that will bring meaning and joy into our lives. In a real sense a grief experience is a "Gethsemane" where we are brought face to face with the necessity of saying: "Here is what I want. Nevertheless, not my will but thine be done." Only what we give up in this way can we truly keep, and herein was the secret of Job's recovery. In the last chapter of the biblical account we see him repenting, that is, changing his mind from resentment to gratitude, from despair about the future to hope. Then, according to the story, twice as much was restored to him as he had ever had before. This does not mean Job got back the same children or the same possessions or the same health, but what he did get back was a deepened and enlarged capacity for life—for gratitude, for sensitivity, for flexibility, and for trust.

I honestly believe that this can happen to any person as a result of the grief process. But there is nothing automatic about it. The experience of loss can embitter a person forever. One can become curdled and resentful against God and the universe and spend the rest of one's days in defiant rage. Or grief can harden and isolate a person. I have known people who have experienced the pain of loss who say: "Never again. I will not make myself vulnerable to this kind of agony." Then, closing themselves off from everyone and everything, they become shriveled and lifeless.

But if we are willing, the experience of grief can deepen and widen our ability to participate in life. We can become more grateful for the gifts we have been given, more openhanded in our handling of the events of life, more sensitive to the whole mysterious process of life, and more trusting in our adventure with God.

And this, of course, is my hope for today's sermon—that it will open the way for you to deal creatively with grief, and in making the best of it, let it in turn make the best of you. The description of the servant in Isaiah is the description of every one of us. From our earliest days we are all persons of sorrow. We are all acquainted with grief. How can we learn to cope with it creatively and not destructively? I have found Job's experience to be a classic pattern. Together we have traced out its course—the numbness and shock, the feeling of utter despair that denies the future, the excursion into nostalgia with the temptation to live there, the feelings of anger and resentment when one tries to understand what has happened. Every griever has had to walk this way.

But let us not stop there. When Job got all the way down to God—to the One with whom we ultimately have to deal—he was there given the grace to see both the past and the future differently. What were these values he had loved and lost? Gifts he had never deserved in the first place. And what about the future? The One from whom had come "the good old days" could be trusted to provide "good new days." If yesterday was so full of meaning, why not tomorrow? All the days come from the same Source! This is how Job moved through his grief—in fact, emerged twice the person he had been.

And so can we! No matter what the form of grief, we can win through and become deeper and richer human beings. No one ever said this would be easy to do, but believe me, it is possible. Job has shown us the way. So, come, people of sorrow, acquainted with grief, let us all follow him and be blessed!

Author

John R. Claypool is an Episcopal priest and a popular preacher, speaker, and retreat leader. He has written ten books, including *The Hopeful Heart*, and is the recipient of four honorary degrees. He currently teaches at Mercer University in Atlanta and divides his time between his residences in Atlanta and New Orleans. John grew up in Nashville, Tennessee, and holds degrees from Mars Hill College, Baylor University, Southern Baptist Theological Seminary, and The Episcopal Theological Seminary of the Southwest.